Valerie Prideaux

Tumbler Quilts

Just One Shape, Endless Possibilities, Play with Color & Design

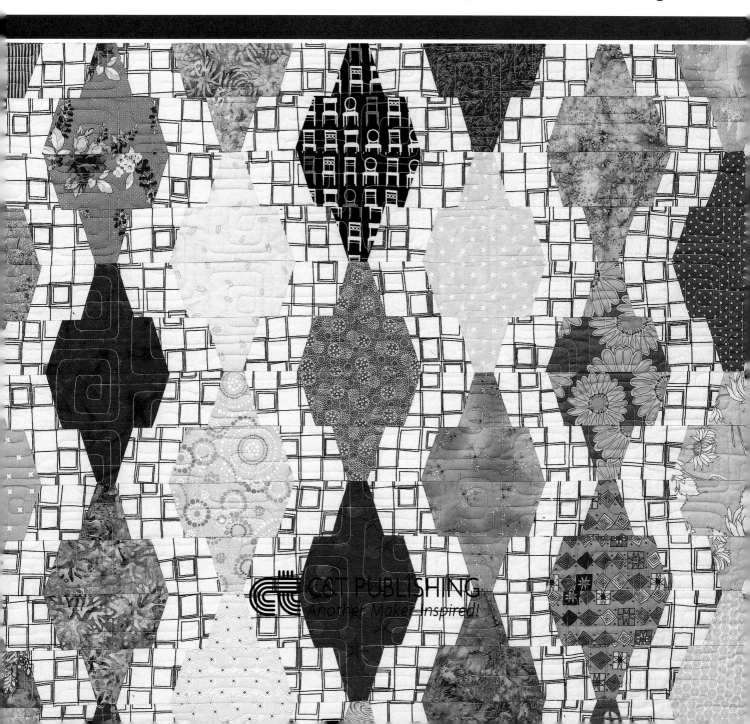

C&T PUBLISHING
Another Maker Inspired!

Text copyright © 2023 by Valerie Prideaux

Photography and artwork copyright © 2023 by C&T Publishing, Inc.

Publisher: Amy Barrett-Daffin

Creative Director: Gailen Runge

Senior Editor: Roxane Cerda

Technical Editor: Debbie Rodgers

Cover/Book Designer: April Mostek

Production Coordinator: Zinnia Heinzmann

Illustrator: Mary E. Flynn

Photography Coordinator: Rachel Ackley

Front cover photography by Bernard Buchanan

Instructional photography by Valerie Prideaux, unless otherwise noted

Published by C&T Publishing, Inc., P.O. Box 1456, Lafayette, CA 94549

Library of Congress Cataloging-in-Publication Data

Names: Prideaux, Valerie, 1948- author.

Title: Tumbler quilts : just one shape, endless possibilities, play with color & design / Valerie Prideaux.

Description: Lafayette, CA : C&T Publishing, [2023] | Summary: "Create everything from simple layouts to art quilts with just one block and a design wall! In this book, Valerie teaches quilters basic design concepts, how to alter tumbler shapes to expand design possibilities and group tumblers to create complex repeated patterns, and color placement for stunning quilts"-- Provided by publisher.

Identifiers: LCCN 2023014353 | ISBN 9781644033777 (trade paperback) | ISBN 9781644033784 (ebook)

Subjects: LCSH: Patchwork--Patterns. | Quilting--Patterns. | Tumbler quilts.

Classification: LCC TT835 .P735 2023 | DDC 746.46/041--dc23/eng/20230418

LC record available at https://lccn.loc.gov/2023014353

Printed in China

10 9 8 7 6 5 4 3 2 1

Dedication

To Charlotte and Hannah with much love.

Acknowledgments

I would like to thank Bernard Buchanan for the terrific job he did with the photography of my quilts, and Roxane Cerda of C&T Publishing for making this whole book writing process as straightforward and painless as she did. A special thanks goes out to Sandy Lindal Beintema of Scrappy Gal Quilt Co for friendship, advice and encouragement. She also quilted most of the quilts in this book—I couldn't have done this without her. Other quilts were quilted by myself and Deb Kopeschny of BloomingLife.ca. And of course, a special thanks to Brian Roberts, for everything.

CONTENTS

Introduction 6

How it All Began 6

Why Tumbler Quilts 7

The Basics 8

Color Play 9

CONTRAST 9

VALUE 10

COLOR SCHEMES 11

Monochromatic 11

Analogous 12

Complementary 14

Neutrals 16

Found Combinations 17

FINAL CONSIDERATIONS 17

Selecting Fabric 18

Getting Started 22

CUTTING 22

USING A DESIGN WALL 22

PIECING THE QUILT TOP 23

Finishing the Quilt 24

SQUARING THE QUILT TOP 24

MAKING THE QUILT SANDWICH 24

QUILTING 25

BINDING 26

PROJECTS

STARTING SIMPLE 28

EIGHT TOGETHER 44

ADDING A SPACER 54

FROM THE BED TO THE WALL 61

Template Patterns 77

About the Author 80

STARTING SIMPLE 28

Peaches and Cream 29

Tumbling Diamonds 32

EIGHT TOGETHER 44   *Working with A and B Blocks 44*

Pink Lemonade 45

Not Just Black and White 48

FROM THE BED TO THE WALL 61

Fire 62

Forest 65

Lava Blue   35

Blue Grotto   38

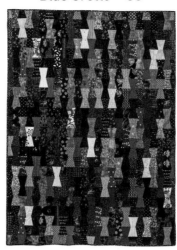

Softly Tumbling   41

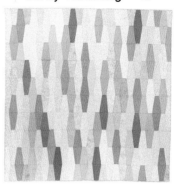

ADDING A SPACER   54   *Working with Spacer Blocks   54*

Getting Your Stripes On   51

Baby Blue   55

Magenta Jam   58

BONUS PROJECT

Blue Ocean   68

Sunrise   71

Come Play With Me   74

Introduction

If you were drawn to quilting because you love color and fabric, single-block quilts are a perfect way to jump right in! What could be easier than a single block and simple piecing? Using just the tumbler block you will be able to cut your fabrics and immediately begin playing on your design wall and create quilts you will love forever.

How it All Began

My love of quilts and quilting begins and ends with color. I've always LOVED color. There were five children in our family, and my mother gave us each a different colored bath towel. I loved seeing them all lined up on the clothesline! I delighted in those boxes with 72 different crayons, and I was thrilled with a coloring book that had an image of Joseph and his coat of many colors.

My working life was in research in science. This work encourages experimenting; always learning, making changes, and trying new things, and this carried over to my life outside of work. I have always had a creative endeavor on the side.

I came to quilting through a long, roundabout way. There were no quilters in the family, and I don't think I saw a quilt until I was in my 30s. I discovered Kaffe Fassett when he published his first knitting book and was inspired by his bright, bold use of pattern and design. I set up a part-time knitting business designing and selling sweater kits for babies and children. This was before digital cameras, color photocopies, and online sales. It was so satisfying creatively, but also very time-consuming. Kaffe moved into quilting, and I got interested. Then a new quilt shop opened near me, and I kept dropping by to have a look at all the fabric. I decided to take the plunge and sold my yarn stock to make room for fabric. Right from the start I was drawn to simple designs that let me play with color.

Why Tumbler Quilts

I have been quilting for about 15 years and have never followed a pattern. I just can't! I may start to, but I get diverted and begin to change things, move them around, and end up with something different from the original. I love that quilting allows me to play endlessly with no judgment.

When my son and his wife were expecting my first grandchild, I wanted to make something special. Parents no longer tuck their babies in with quilts at nap time but use one-piece sleepers. Quilts are for tummy time, nursery decoration, or tucked around the baby for warmth when they are in a stroller or car seat.

I quickly decided to make a baby quilt that could be placed on the floor or hung on the wall in the baby's room. My stash had a lot of novelty prints, some especially suited for children, others just fun. Does a baby need a quilt with images of glasses or a typewriter? No, but the parents would probably get a kick out of it! Though I love "I Spy" quilts, I find them too busy. I remembered a tumbler template I had on hand, played with that, and haven't looked back. To make your own version of this baby quilt, *Come Play with Me*, flip to the bonus project at the end of the book (page 74).

I was inspired to try a traditional tumbler quilt and quickly realized how versatile this block could be; how it allowed me to move blocks around on my design wall to create different designs, try different layouts, and play with color. What an exciting journey this has been!

Quilts aren't just for sleeping!

THE BASICS

Anyone can enjoy making tumbler block quilts, whether you are a beginner who wants to start simple, an advanced quilter who wants a palette cleanser between more complicated projects, or just someone who loves color. The quilts in this book allow you to play with design and color but are beginner-friendly because most of them use only one block. The variety you can get just by playing with the arrangement of blocks on your design wall is pretty incredible.

Are you ready to take the plunge into tumbler quilts? Starting a new project can be intimidating, but the simplest way to begin is to consider what fabrics and colors you would like to use and start cutting. With this type of quilt, you are simply cutting blocks from fabric and putting them on the design wall. You are not committed to using them in the final piece. Since most of the quilts in this book use just a single size of tumbler template each, you can always save unused blocks for another quilt!

Pick some fabrics, cut blocks, place your blocks on the design wall, move them around, and assemble: You'll have a finished quilt in no time. The next section will show you some of the traditional ways that these blocks are used in a quilt but remember that traditional doesn't have to mean boring!

Tumbling Diamonds, variation (page 32)

Color Play

Are you wondering where to start? If this step worries you, you are not alone! I suggest choosing a design that inspires you, and then a color scheme that you are drawn to.

Contrast

First, try to determine if you want a lot of contrast in your quilt, or if you want a more blended look. Bold contrast grabs attention, while a subtle or gradual contrast draws you in as your eye follows the transitions. The mostly black and white quilt, at right, features bold contrast, while the use of mid-range striped fabrics gives a very different look to a similar arrangement of blocks.

Not Just Black and White (page 48)

Getting Your Stripes On (page 51)

Bold versus blended contrast in similar layouts

Detail of *Sunrise* (page 71)

Detail in *Not Just Black and White*

Areas of high and low contrast in quilts

Look at the quilts in this book for more examples of bold and subtle transitions. Start taking note of which quilts appeal most to you and what type of contrast they use. You don't need to decide now, just keep this in mind when you are ready to start playing on the design wall.

Using a color wheel can be a great way to make color choices for your tumbler quilt, so let's have a closer look.

Value

In the color wheel on the right, you'll notice that most color wheels have rings of color. The outer ring shows pure colors. The next ring in shows the tint (the color with white added), the next ring in from that shows the tones (the color with gray added), and the center ring shows the shade (the color with black added). This is called the color's intensity, or value.

In short, value refers to the relative lightness or darkness of a color. When values match, for example, colors with light values are placed together, they tend to blend. However, when values are mixed, meaning light value and dark value colors are placed together, they really stand out. The images below show a group of blocks with all light-value tumblers and another with group with all dark-value tumblers. The third illustration shows these values mixed together. In the mixed values example, notice how the darker tumblers catch your eye and define the pattern in the piece. If you want a high-contrast quilt, you might place the dark blocks first, and find a pleasing arrangement. Then add in the lighter blocks.

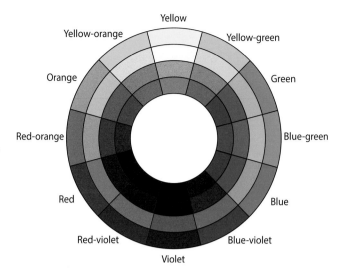

Here are some examples of blocks with similar values, but different colors. Each of these sets would be considered low contrast because the values or intensities are similar. Remember, just because a color is bright or dark, if there aren't mixed color values in the quilt, it is still a low-contrast quilt.

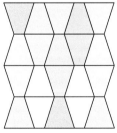

Light values

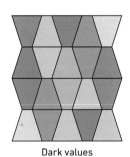

Dark values

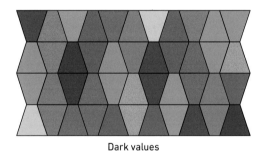

Dark values

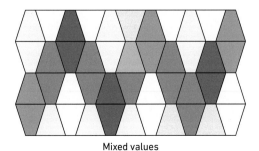

Mixed values

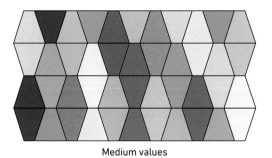

Medium values

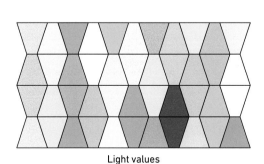

Light values

Color Schemes

There are so many different ways to combine colors that you can easily feel overwhelmed. Thinking of how colors relate to each other can help you choose the colors for your quilt and knowing just a few of these relationships is a great place to start. There are many different ways to combine colors, but there are a few simple tried-and-true schemes that will always yield good results. Most of my quilts use a monochromatic, analogous, or complementary color scheme. Let's learn more about these combinations.

MONOCHROMATIC

A monochromatic color scheme uses just one color but includes tints (the color with white added), tones (the color with gray added), and shades (the color with black added) of that color.

Using the tints, tones, and shades gives you so many options, and since they are all variations on one color they are sure to go together. For example, you can separate similar values for a bolder look or organize them in a gradation for a softer look.

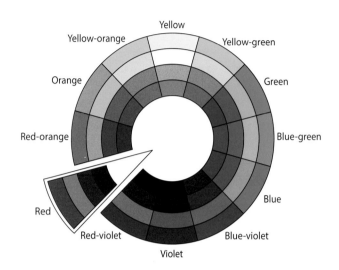

A blue monochromatic color scheme

Detail of *Blue Ocean* (page 68) featuring a wide range of blues.

ANALOGOUS

An analogous color scheme uses colors that are next to one another on the color wheel, for example yellow, orange, and pink.

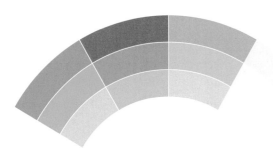

The fabrics below show a range of analogous colors, from yellow to orange, to red.

It is important to still consider color values when using an analogous color scheme. These blocks use analogous colors, but they are similar in value.

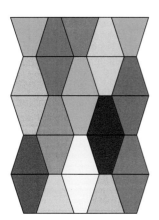

Various tints and tones have been added to these blocks and, as a result, are much more successful. Because there is a range of values in these blocks there is more movement and the arrangement becomes more interesting.

The two quilts below and on the right are examples of an analogous color scheme. They each use a range of values of analogous colors; in this case red, orange, and yellow. If the quilts had used similar values of each of the colors used, they would have been less successful.

The wide band of white around the colors in *Fire* (page 62) cools the hot color scheme down,
and gives the eye a place to rest, making this the more eye-catching quilt.

COMPLEMENTARY

A complementary color scheme is very different from the previous schemes, but still very effective. This scheme uses two colors which are directly across from one another on the color wheel and gives the most contrast of any color scheme. Examples are red and green, orange and blue, or yellow and purple, with one of the two colors chosen as the dominant one. When you play with value by adding tints, tones, and shades of those colors, you have a lot of options, and can be assured that they will harmonize.

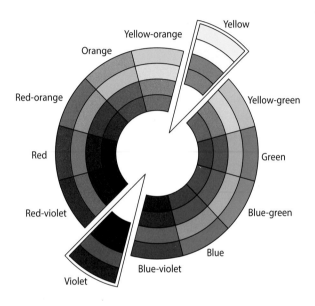

Yellow and violet are opposites on the color wheel so they are considered complementary colors.

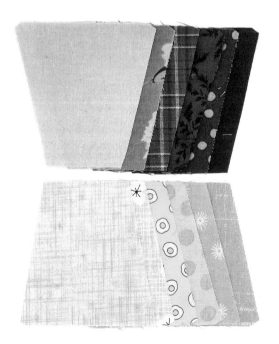

Blue Grotto (page 38) uses a complementary color scheme. While orange is considered the complement of blue, here the blues are dark, and veering towards purple, and the yellow blocks work as a contrast.

It is more effective if you choose one color to be dominant. This set of blocks features a red-green complementary color scheme with mostly red blocks with shots of green.

This set of blocks also uses a red-green combination, but has a balance of red and green and, to my eye, is less effective.

There are more color schemes, but as you page through this book, you'll see that most of my quilts use a monochromatic, analogous, or complementary color scheme. If choosing colors is challenging, I suggest you refer back to the color wheel and start with one of these color schemes. They all make great quilts.

Blue Grotto

NEUTRALS

Notice there are no whites, grays, or blacks on the color wheel. These are considered neutral colors and are a great secret weapon for quilters. They go with any color they are paired with, and can be added to, any color scheme. Neutrals extend your choices of color and are a go-to for many quilters. If you feel your quilt is "too much"—too bold, too bright, too busy, you can't go wrong adding them to your design!

Tumbling Diamonds (page 32) is a simple yet effective quilt because the neutrals really make the blocks that form the diamonds stand out.

Notice how the colors in *Forest,* below, fade to neutral near the edges of the quilt, drawing your eye into the darker areas of the quilt. The central area of the quilt is an analogous scheme of yellow-green-blue.

Forest (page 65)

Tumbling Diamonds (page 32)

FOUND COMBINATIONS

There are lots of other places to find color combinations. Web designers have long played with color to create a mood for their sites, so websites are a great source of color inspiration. Paint companies have all those wonderful paint chips that you can pick up for free and many of these chips have color combinations on the back for more ideas. Another resource I have used is Joen Wolfram's *Ultimate 3-in-1 Color Tool*, which offers 37 variations of a color on each card. On the flip side are 5 different combinations, showing coordinating and contrasting colors from the color wheel.

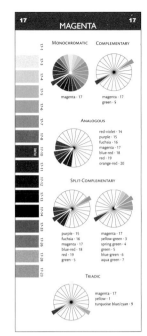

An example from Joen Wolfram's book, shows the possibilities for using the color magenta.

And finally, don't be afraid to borrow a combination you like from other quilts that you see online or in person. Most of all, be adventurous! If you see a color combination that you think works, cut some blocks and put them on your design wall. If you decide you love it, keep going! If you change your mind, move those blocks away and try others, or think about adding lighter or darker shades of one or more colors. Check the color wheel for ideas. Lighter, darker, more contrast, or less? This is the fun and creative part of your quiltmaking, so don't be afraid to play with lots of possibilities before you start sewing blocks together.

Final Considerations

When you see a quilt you love, think about why. What keeps you looking at that quilt? What catches your eye first, and then what other elements draw you in after that? The most interesting quilts have movement, and that is what draws your eye in and around the quilt. The shape of the tumbler block itself creates a sense of movement. Movement also comes from color contrast and value changes. Gradual contrast leads the eye from one area to another slowly, while high contrast pulls your eye in immediately.

Is there a specific color you like? If yes, focus on it. Do you want to make your quilt in a narrow color range or use lots and lots of different colors? Remember, you can play with different possibilities on your design wall until you are happy. Playing with color is really my favorite part of quiltmaking.

One final thing to consider in your quilt is adding a surprise element. This may be the first thing you notice when looking at a quilt, or you might see it later when spending more time examining it—either way these surprise elements will definitely intrigue the viewer. Tiny flashes of white in some of the darker blue fabrics, and a violet block amongst the dark purples are surprise elements in *Blue Ocean,* below.

Blue Ocean (page 68)

Selecting Fabric

Now that you have a color scheme in mind it is time to select fabrics. I use print fabrics in most of my quilts: They offer an endless variety of possibilities. Print fabrics are what drew me to quilting, from that first visit to a quilt shop.

For the color variation of *Magenta Jam* (page 58) I loved the floral fabric in the center of the blocks and chose an analogous color scheme of red-orange-yellow for the tumbler blocks surrounding the print itself.

Magenta Jam, floral version (page 58)

I could have easily chosen a monochromatic red scheme instead.

The printed design on a fabric may be similar in color to the background of the fabric, or it may contrast. If there is contrast, the print can catch your eye and draw you in, but if the design is more uniform the fabrics can appear to blend from one block to the next. Batiks, tone-on-tone, and smaller prints work best for gradual transitions. The pieces to the right are in the same color family but feature a multi-colored print, one with a more subtle design, and one that is a tone-on-tone.

I feature a few quilts in this book that use only solid fabrics. The finished look of these quilts is quite different from those that use patterned fabric, where colors flow more easily one to the next. The blocks of color in these quilts are quite distinct from each other and this gives a crisp look to the finished piece. Take a closer look and decide which appeals to you!

Magenta Jam (page 58) is made entirely from solids.

Because I usually work in fairly narrow color ranges I rely on value, movement, and texture to provide interest in my quilts. The shape of the tumbler block itself helps move your eye around the quilt and the quilting adds texture.

By blending slowly from dark to light groups of blocks this alternate colorway of *Pink Lemonade* (page 45) features a lot of movement.

Detail of *Baby Blue* (page 55). The quilting adds movement to the finished look.

TIPS FOR FINDING FABRICS

▶ Start with Stash
Looking through your fabric stash can be a great starting point. Maybe you have a fat quarter bundle or a charm pack you are eager to use. If so, a lot of color choices have already been made by the fabric designer. You may need more fabrics to make your quilt, so look for coordinating fabrics with similar but not exact color matches. This will add interest to your quilt.

▶ Fabric From Friends
Are you in a quilt guild or have friends that quilt? If yes, put the word out that you are looking for small pieces of fabric in particular colors. Give approximate dimensions for the size of fabric that you need. For example, 4″ × 8″ is more than enough for two small tumblers. You'll be surprised how generous quilters can be!

Let the Fabric Do the Work

One way to keep your design decisions simple but interesting is to let the fabric do the talking. Charm squares are a great way to begin working with tumbler blocks and build your first quilt. Find a pack that features a color you like, combine it with a neutral solid, and get started.

Another solution is to use ombre fabrics. Just select two ombre fabrics in related colors and you are ready to go. Check out *Peaches and Cream* (page 29), it uses a few charm packs and an off-white fabric.

The ombre runner below uses just two different ombre fabrics.

Both of these approaches make fabric selection easy.

Peaches and Cream (page 29) uses charm squares.

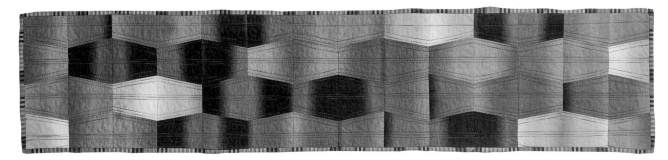

One last note on fabric choices. I have a lot of boldly colored large prints in my fabric stash. They are stunning but can be difficult to use in this type of quilt. Cutting a row of blocks from one of these fabrics can result in unpredictably colored blocks. There are so many projects available that highlight these fabrics better, so save the large prints for those.

Are you worried that you don't have enough fabrics? Turn your fabric over and look at the back. Many fabrics will work perfectly as a lighter version of the color you are using. You may think the blocks look "wrong" when piecing your quilt, but when the quilt is completed, you won't even notice—promise!

Right and wrong side of the same fabric. Check the back of your fabrics: The lighter tint you are looking for might be right in front of you!

Getting Started

Cutting

Now it's time to start cutting blocks. Decide which project you are interested in. Each project uses one or more templates to cut out your blocks. You will find the template patterns at the end of the book. The required seam allowance for each block is built into the template, so a 3½″ tall template will result in blocks that will be 3″ tall and a template that is 5″ tall will finish at 4½″ after being pieced.

If you are making a scrappy quilt you'll only need one or two blocks per fabric so you can utilize small scraps of fabric. Most designs in this book call for lots of different fabrics, so you won't need many blocks from any one fabric.

If you want multiple tumbler blocks from a fabric, the most efficient way to cut several blocks is to cut a long strip the width of the fabric (WOF), usually 40″ to 42″ of useable fabric, then use a template to sub-cut the tumblers. Templates A, B, and C are each 3½″ in height so you would need a strip 3½″ × WOF. Template D is 5″ tall so you would a strip 5″ × WOF.

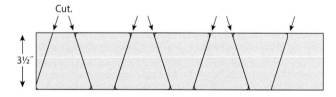

▶ Just a Little Fabric
One rectangle 3½″ × 40″ WOF yields 15 template A tumbler blocks. If using one fat quarter, you can cut approximately 35 tumbler blocks using template A. Remember, you can save your leftover blocks for another project.

Take a look at the template patterns at the back of the book. Notice the trimmed corners. When you are cutting out your tumbler blocks, be sure not to skip trimming these corners. The trimmed corners help the pieces fit together perfectly when sewing blocks together, and this helps keep your rows straight, an important step in piecing your quilt. Without these trimmed corners, you would have an ⅛″ piece of fabric at each end when two blocks are sewn together and this would need to be trimmed to keep your rows straight.

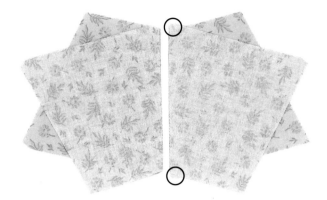

Untrimmed tumbler blocks (right) require trimming, the trimmed blocks (left) do not.

Another option for the technically minded is to use a digital cutter such as AccuQuilt, Sizzix, or Cricut. Most come with a standard tumbler template, and more advanced machines allow you to program in the shapes you want to cut.

Using a Design Wall

A design wall is an important element in designing your quilt. It may sound like something fancy and expensive, but it's not! Most people make a design wall by simply taping a large piece of batting to a wall. The blocks will adhere to the batting but can still be easily moved about. Viewing your blocks straight-on, rather than laying them on a bed or the floor, gives a better view of your work in progress. Finally, you want to be able to stand back about six to eight feet as you work on your quilt to get a sense of whether or not it is coming together as you hoped.

Once you've cut your blocks, start moving them to your design wall. Take time to play with the arrangement of your blocks. Stand back and look at your work so far. Do you like the colors you have chosen? If not, try re-arranging them or swapping in other fabrics. Do you like the original better? Taking a photo of your trial layouts often helps to choose your favorite.

Do they contrast or blend enough? A helpful tip is to take photos of your work in progress and convert them to black and white. The contrast and blending are more obvious in this format and allow you to identify any problem areas. When you are happy with your fabrics and layout choices, it is time to start sewing.

Lava Blue (page 35)

A photo of the quilt converted to grayscale.

Piecing the Quilt Top

When piecing I use a scant ¼″ seam for accuracy and I always use 50-weight thread to reduce bulk. Be careful at this stage. Tumbler blocks have angled sides, and thus two sides of your blocks have bias edges which can easily stretch. Avoid handling the fabric too much and use pins to secure the sides before sewing. Press with your iron, do not use a back-and-forth motion. Begin piecing the blocks together, sewing the long edge of one block to another, and be sure that on the top and bottom of each pair you have one wider edge and one narrower edge.

To keep your blocks in the correct order, work with 2 blocks at a time and replace them on the design wall before sewing the next pair. Continue sewing the blocks sets together in pairs, then sew these pairs to one another in the correct order.

To keep the row straight, I like to line up a completed row on my ironing board along a straight edge, such as a ruler. Press using the straight edge as a guide, adjusting as needed. Apply a shot of steam, let the fabric cool, and voila, a straight edge. Accuracy at this point will prevent problems later! Press all of the seams in a row in one direction. For example, all seams in the first row can be pressed to the right. The seams of the next row should be pressed in the opposite direction. Continue piecing and pressing until all your rows are finished.

Use a straight line to maintain accuracy.

Start sewing your rows together, two at a time. Because you pressed the seams in each row in opposite directions, they should nest together easily. Once all the rows are sewn together, press seams between rows in one direction. I press these upward, but you may prefer to press them open to reduce bulk. Continue sewing rows together until your quilt top is complete.

Finishing the Quilt

Now that your quilt top has been assembled, you are ready for the next steps. These include squaring up your quilt top so that each corner is a 90° angle and the quilt will lie flat and adding a layer of batting and a background fabric to create a quilt sandwich. The final steps are quilting your quilt sandwich, squaring it up again, and adding the binding.

Squaring the Quilt Top

Due to the shape of the blocks, you will have uneven edges along both sides of your quilt, or the top and bottom if the design is rotated. Once all the rows are sewn together, trim these sides to square the quilt up, leaving partial blocks at the edges.

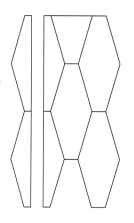

The first step in squaring your quilt top is to press the top well, to be sure it lies flat, with no bumps or folds. If you have a floor with square tiles, tape your quilt top to the floor, using the tiles as a guide. You can also do this on your design wall. Measure the width of your quilt at the top, bottom and middle to see how much adjustment you need to make. Use a water-soluble blue marker to mark a line where you need to trim the sides of the quilt, move to your work table and trim as needed.

Repeat this, measuring the height of the quilt at the sides and middle of your quilt. Another option is to use a large, square ruler, align it with the top edge of the quilt. Align another ruler against this one down the length of the quilt, and trim first one side of the quilt, then the other. Repeat for the top and bottom edges of your quilt top. You will be squaring up the entire quilt in the same way after it is quilted.

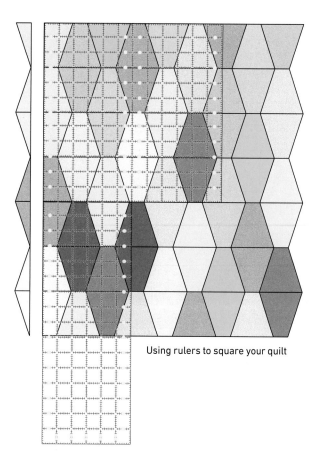

Using rulers to square your quilt

Making the Quilt Sandwich

You will need batting and a backing fabric to complete your quilt. Each of these should be at least 4″ wider than your quilt top at both sides, top and bottom.

Start by laying the quilt backing right side down—you can do this on the floor, a table, or tape it to a wall if your table is too small. Center the batting over the backing, smoothing out any folds or bumps. Finally, center your quilt top over the batting right side up, again smoothing out any wrinkles or folds. Repeat the process of squaring up the quilt, checking that the corners and edges are square. No trimming this time. You must secure these three layers together. Many quilters use safety pins, secured at regular intervals, while others choose to use a temporary adhesive between each layer of the sandwich. Still others hand baste the layers together. Make one final check that both the front and back of your quilt sandwich are free of any bumps or tucks. Your sandwich is now ready to be quilted!

Quilting

The final thing you need to consider for your project is how to quilt the quilt! Quilting adds texture and helps bring it all together. Some simple but effective ideas to consider are straight lines, following the lines of tumbler blocks, and curvy lines. Quilts with lots of patterned fabrics are a great place to use simple allover patterns. It can sometimes be difficult to work out what the quilting design is in this type of quilt, so keep it simple. Quilts made from solid fabrics, especially darker solids, show the quilting well, so this is the place to splash out on fun interesting quilting designs. As you look more closely at the quilts in this book, remember to look at the quilting. I've tried to include a variety of patterns to inspire you.

Several quilting patterns to consider

Binding

Quilters often say binding a quilt is their least favorite part of the quilt making process. If this is you, remember that once this is done, your quilt is complete, ready to gift or to snuggle under. Choose a fabric that contrasts or coordinates with your quilt. It's up to you!

I use a generous 2½″ wide strip of fabric to create a single-fold binding at the quilt edge. This gives a narrow binding on the front of the quilt, and a wider binding on the back. I love this look! To find how much fabric you will need in length, first calculate the total circumference of your quilt.

For a 60″ × 80″ quilt:

60 + 80 + 60 + 80″ = 280″

Add 12″ to this measurement, for a total of 292″.

Cut enough strips to get this length and join into one continuous strip. You will need the extra inches we added for seams and to create neat, mitered corners.

Fold a ½″ seam at the starting edge of your binding and lay the binding strip along the perimeter of the quilt, right sides together. Sew the binding to the quilt with a ¼″ seam, stopping ¼″ from the corner. Fold the binding strip up at the corner of the binding strip, creating a 90° angle at the corner of the quilt. Now fold the strip down, so the top edge is aligned with the edge you have just finished sewing. Your binding strip is now aligned to the next side of your quilt.

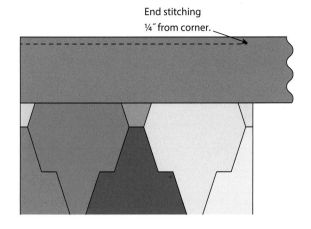

End stitching ¼″ from corner.

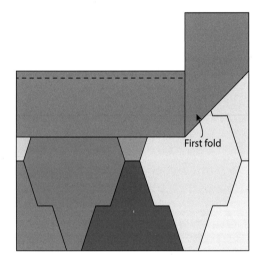

First fold

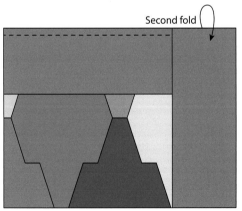

Second fold

Binding corners of your quilt

Continue in this manner around the entire quilt. Allow a ½″ overlap with your starting point, and trim excess binding. Finger press your binding up, turn to the back of the quilt, and fold the outer edge of your binding under to the edge of the quilt, creating a double layer. Hand stitch the binding to the back of the quilt.

There are many different ways to bind a quilt. Check out YouTube videos if you want to explore other methods, or if you want to follow along visually step-by-step. Once you've done this a few times you may find it a relaxing thing to do while sitting chatting with friends or watching television. And congratulations—your quilt is now finished!

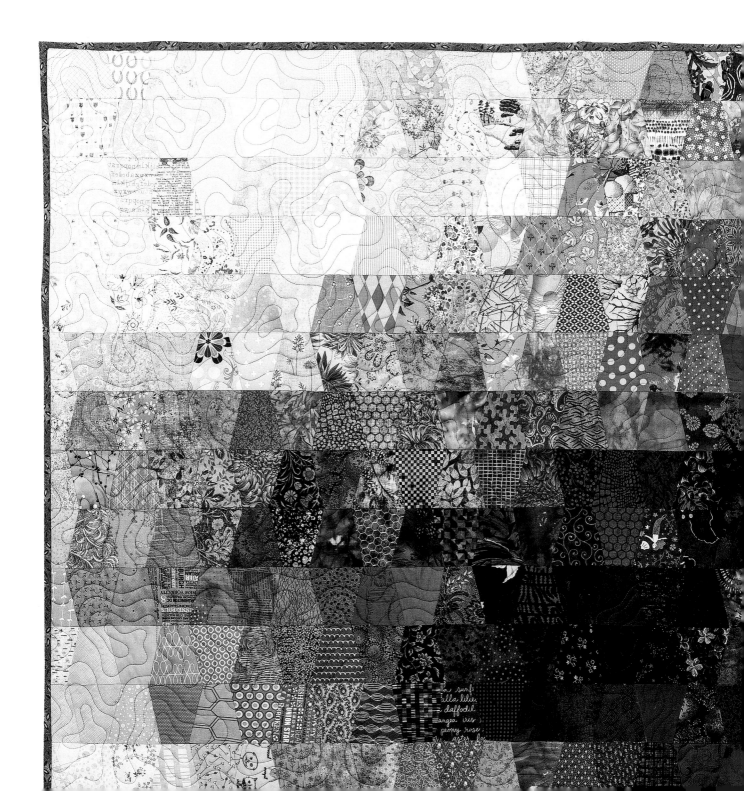

STARTING SIMPLE

I started exploring simple arrangements of tumbler blocks and loved how this instantly allowed me to play with color using my stash of fabrics. The quilts in this chapter use a single template and are a great place to start your tumbler journey. These quilts may be simple, but simple does not have to mean boring!

Peaches and Cream

| FINISHED SIZE: 41″ × 49½″ |

Peaches and Cream is a beginner-friendly quilt design that uses a larger tumbler template and an analogous color scheme mixed with cream; a great place to start your tumbler journey! I was SO attracted to the background color of the fabric that features cats with antlers, and that became the starting point for this quilt. I used a soft version of the analogous color scheme of pink to orange to gold. If you would like to make a larger quilt, simply add more blocks!

This cat print from *The Highlands* by Violet Craft for Michael Miller Fabrics was my starting point.

MATERIALS

Quantities are for 42/44″ wide, 100% cotton fabrics. Measurements include a ¼″ seam allowance.

TEMPLATE D (page 78)

FABRIC A: 66 charm squares or equivalent in 5″ squares, various shades of peach, coral, pink, and orange

FABRIC B: 66 charm squares in various shades of lightly patterned off-white fabric or 1¼ yards of a single fabric

BACKING: 2¾ yards

BINDING: ½ yard coordinating fabric

BATTING: 49″ × 58″

CUTTING THE FABRIC

For tips and tricks on cutting tumbler blocks see Cutting (page 22).

FABRIC A

Trim the 66 squares into tumbler blocks using template D.

FABRIC B

For charm squares: Trim the 66 squares into tumbler blocks using template D.

For yardage: Cut 7 strips 5″ × WOF; subcut 66 tumbler blocks using template D. Each 5″ strip should yield 10 blocks.

► CHANGING IT UP

This is such a simple design that it lends itself to lots of color choices. How about changing the background to a color that coordinates with the main fabric, or one that features spotted fabrics? Choose your favorite and go! Here are some other examples to inspire you.

Monochromatic scheme in a range of greens paired with an off-white fabric.

Similar values in main and background fabric for a soft look.

Piecing the Quilt

1. Place the blocks on your design wall, alternating colored charm squares, Fabric A, with your background fabrics, Fabric B, as shown in the main quilt photo. Spend some time moving your blocks around, trying different arrangements. For guidance on arranging your blocks see Using a Design Wall (page 22).

2. When you are happy with all your fabric choices and your arrangement, it is time to move to your sewing machine. Referring to Piecing the Quilt Top (page 23), begin piecing the blocks together, working with 2 blocks at a time, and replacing them on the design wall.

3. When the row is complete, press the seams in one direction. The seams of the next row should be pressed in the opposite direction. Continue until all your rows are sewn.

4. Check that you have pressed the seams in alternate directions one row to the next, then sew the rows together.

Completing the Quilt

1. Using the guidance in Squaring the Quilt Top (page 24), trim the quilt to eliminate the partial blocks at the sides, and make any adjustments needed to be sure the quilt is squared up.

2. Layer the quilt top, batting, and backing.

3. Quilt as desired. I decided to have this quilted with an all-over design, using a fine white thread. The thread disappears into the blocks and the pattern is more visible on the solid portions of the quilt. For more information see Quilting (page 25).

4. Bind the quilt with a complementary fabric. For a refresher see Binding (page 26).

Why it Works

I used a wide range of soft, analogous colors with similar values for the blocks in this quilt; everything from pink to gold, arranged randomly across the quilt. The neutral background creates space to let each fabric shine.

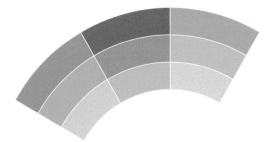

Most colors for this quilt come from the tints in the middle ring

PEACHES AND CREAM

Tumbling Diamonds

| FINISHED SIZE: 45″ × 63″ |

Who doesn't love diamonds? This design idea came from arranging tumbler blocks on my design wall and is a very different look from the previous quilt, but just as simple. Arranging the blocks in a different way gives a totally different look to this quilt; not your average tumbler block quilt!

MATERIALS

Quantities are for 42/44″ wide, 100% cotton fabrics. Measurements include ¼″ seam allowances.

Use the quilt photo as a guide for colors to use.

TEMPLATE A (page 77)

BACKGROUND: 2½ yards or equivalent from various low-volume fabrics

FABRIC A: ½ yard or equivalent from various mid blues

FABRIC B: ½ yard or equivalent from various dark blues

FABRIC C: ⅜ yard or equivalent from various lime greens

FABRIC D: ⅜ yard or equivalent from various light blues

FABRIC E: ¼ yard or equivalent from various light lime greens

BACKING: 3 yards

BINDING: ½ yard coordinating fabric

BATTING: 53″ × 71″

CUTTING THE FABRIC

For tips and tricks on cutting tumbler blocks see Cutting (page 22).

BACKGROUND

Cut 342 tumbler blocks with template A.

FABRIC A

Cut 40 tumbler blocks with template A.

FABRIC B

Cut 44 tumbler blocks with template A.

FABRIC C

Cut 28 tumbler blocks with template A.

FABRIC D

Cut 21 tumbler blocks with template A.

FABRIC E

Cut 8 tumbler blocks with template A.

CHANGING IT UP

This is such a simple design that it lends itself to lots of design possibilities. How about changing the background to something bright and bold? Or, you could try adding more diamonds in the background spaces—or both!

A leaf green background and added diamonds in the corner really make this diamond motif sparkle.

The central diamonds use solid fabrics, creating an interesting contrast to the background, which is made from a wide range of tone-on-tone red fabrics.

Piecing the Quilt

1. Arrange the blocks on your design wall, following the layout in the main quilt photo. For guidance on arranging your blocks see Using a Design Wall (page 22).

2. When you are happy with all your fabric choices and your arrangement, it is time to move to your sewing machine. Referring to Piecing the Quilt Top (page 23), begin piecing the blocks together, working with 2 blocks at a time, and replacing them on the design wall.

3. When the row is complete, press the seams in one direction. The seams of the next row should be pressed in the opposite direction. Continue until all your rows are sewn.

4. Check that you have pressed the seams in alternate directions one row to the next, then sew the rows together.

Completing the Quilt

1. Using the guidance in Squaring the Quilt Top (page 24), trim the quilt to eliminate the partial blocks at the sides, and make any adjustments needed to be sure the quilt is squared up.

2. Layer the quilt top, batting, and backing.

3. Quilt as desired. I used straight-line horizontal quilting on this quilt with lines spaced 1″ apart. It is important that your rows are very straight and parallel if you do horizontal quilting. Consider a different design if your rows wobble. This can happen because you may be quilting on or near the long horizontal seam allowances, which give extra bulk. Vertical straight quilting lines look just as effective and are a lot easier to do! For more information see Quilting (page 25).

4. Bind the quilt with a color that coordinates with the quilt top. For a refresher see Binding (page 26).

Why it Works

I used a range of blue and yellow-green fabrics that were neighbors on the color wheel for this quilt and arranged them to form concentric diamonds. The shape of the blocks adds extra interest to the design. A range of pale neutrals in the background helps to draw your eye in and encourages you to study the quilt more closely.

Lava Blue

| FINISHED SIZE: 41″ × 49½″ |

There is a volcano in Indonesia called Kawah Ijen. The flames from the lava, barely visible by day, are a stunningly beautiful and highly visible blue at night. The colors in the lava inspired this quilt, and fittingly, this arrangement of tumbler blocks is called lava lamp.

MATERIALS

Quantities are for 42/44″ wide, 100% cotton fabrics. Measurements include ¼″ seam allowances.

I used several charm square packs to make this quilt. This is a perfect way to use charm packs, as you don't need much fabric for each block. The fabrics in this quilt feature fabrics with small-scale prints in similar tones to the background, helping them flow from light to dark through placement on the design wall.

TEMPLATE D (page 78)

MAIN FABRIC: 60 pairs of charm squares plus 12 more, or 72 rectangles at least 6″ × 10″, or ⅛ yard of 72 fabrics ranging from white with a touch of blue to light, medium, and dark blue

BACKING: 2¾ yards

BINDING: ½ yard of coordinating fabric

BATTING: 49″ × 58″

CUTTING THE FABRIC

For tips and tricks on cutting tumbler blocks see Cutting (page 22).

MAIN FABRIC

Cut 60 pairs of tumbler blocks from 2 identical squares, a rectangle, or yardage using template D.

Cut 12 individual tumbler blocks from the remaining squares, rectangles, or yardage using template D.

Piecing the Quilt

1. Play with the placement of your blocks on your design wall. Refer to the main quilt image for quilt block placement. Add your pairs of tumbler blocks, with wider ends together, and build from the darkest blues outward, starting slightly off center. For guidance on arranging your blocks see Using a Design Wall (page 22).

2. When you are happy with all your fabric choices and your arrangement, it is time to move to your sewing machine. Begin piecing the blocks together, working with 2 blocks at a time, and replacing them on the design wall.

►CHANGING IT UP

Using the same basic layout, but with a magenta-purple ombre colorway gives a totally new look. What colors would you use?

For a totally different look, I created this table runner using template A, and the same lava lamp layout. The fact that it is so stunning, yet so simple, is the result of the gradations in color in the original fabric. This runner uses only a ½ yard each of 2 ombre fabrics with similar color gradations. Notice how the quilting lines follow the shapes of the tumbler blocks. This runner would make a great gift!

Rows are 12 blocks wide. Referring to Piecing the Quilt Top (page 23).

3. When the row is complete, press the seams in one direction. The seams of the next row should be pressed in the opposite direction.

4. Continue until all your rows are sewn. Check that you have pressed the seams in alternate directions from one row to the next, then sew rows together.

Completing the Quilt

1. Using the guidance in Squaring the Quilt Top (page 24), trim the edges of the quilt straight to square the quilt.

2. Layer the quilt top, batting, and backing.

3. Quilt as desired I chose an all-over quilting design for this quilt, and it was quilted with a light blue thread. The quilt pattern is almost invisible in the darker areas of the quilt but can be more easily seen in the lighter areas, giving textural and visual interest. For more information see Quilting (page 25).

4. Add a complementary binding. For a refresher see Binding (page 26).

Why it Works

I believe this quilt works because of the ombre effect created by fabric placement and the movement it creates. Your eye is immediately drawn to the darker area of the quilt, which has been placed off-center rather than right in the middle. Your eye then follows the ombre effect outward to the edges of the quilt.

Blue Grotto

| FINISHED QUILT SIZE: 49″ × 72″ |

There is a lovely sea cave on the Isle of Capri in Italy named the Grotta Azzurra, or Blue Grotto. The further you venture into the cave, the deeper the blues, with small spots of sunshine sparkling on the water. The darker shades of blue in this quilt remind me of that magical place. This quilt was made using pairs of tumbling blocks from a wide range of fabrics, mostly from my stash. The blocks are arranged with the narrowest edges touching and is often called the hourglass layout.

MATERIALS

Quantities are for 42/44″ wide, 100% cotton fabrics. Measurements include ¼″ seam allowances.

TEMPLATE A (page 77)

BLUES: 291 rectangles at least 4″ × 7″, or ⅛ yard each of 85 mid to dark blue fabrics

BRIGHT YELLOWS: ⅛ yard each of 3 fabrics

BACKING: 3¼ yards

BINDING: ⅝ yard

BATTING: 58″ × 80″

CUTTING THE FABRIC

For tips and tricks on cutting tumbler blocks see Cutting (page 22).

BLUES

Cut 294 pairs of tumbler blocks using template A. Cut 3 or 4 pairs from each fabric if using ⅛ yard cuts.

BRIGHT YELLOWS

Cut 3 pairs of tumbler blocks from each yellow using template A, for a total of 18 tumbler blocks.

Piecing the Quilt

1. Refer to the main quilt image for quilt block placement. Play with your blocks on the design wall until you are happy with the layout. Remember to sprinkle the yellow tumbler block pairs throughout the quilt randomly. For the first row, you will alternate a single block with a full pair, as shown in the quilt photograph. You can use the other half of the pair in the bottom row of the quilt. For guidance on arranging your blocks see Using a Design Wall (page 22).

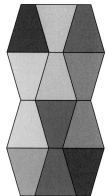

2. Now it is time to move to your sewing machine. Working with 2 blocks at a time, piece the blocks together and replace them on the design wall. Rows are 25 blocks across, and 24 down. Referring to Piecing the Quilt Top (page 23).

3. When the row is complete, press the seams in one direction. The seams of the next row should be pressed in the opposite direction.

4. Continue until all your rows are sewn. Check that you have pressed the seams in alternate directions one row to the next, then sew rows together.

Completing the Quilt

1. Using the guidance in Squaring the Quilt Top (page 24), trim the quilt, checking that the quilt is square.

2. Layer the quilt top, batting, and backing.

3. Quilt as desired. I decided to have this quilted with a loopy design in each tumbler pair, using a fine blue thread. The thread disappears into the blue blocks and is slightly visible on the yellow blocks of the quilt, but does not detract from the overall look. For more information see Quilting (page 25).

4. Bind the quilt with a complementary fabric. For a refresher see Binding (page 26).

Why it Works

This quilt uses a narrow range of darker blue fabrics, and blue is considered a cool color. The bright yellow is from the warm side of the color wheel, and it is this contrast that makes this quilt work. Yellow is not quite complementary to blue (orange is), but the cool-warm contrast and deep intensity of both colors, plus the limited amount of yellow really catch your eye and brighten the look of this quilt.

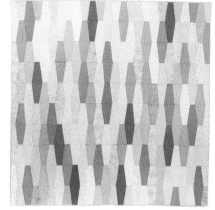

Softly Tumbling

| FINISHED SIZE: 77″ × 80″ |

A friend of mine loves soft, muted colors in her quilts, and that idea inspired me to make this quilt. I don't have a lot of these lighter tints and tones in my stash, so I headed to a local shop and bought ¼ yard cuts of a bunch of fabrics. Not until the quilt was completed, on my bed, and the lights turned out did I learn I had bought some glow-in-the-dark fabrics!

MATERIALS

Quantities are for 42/44″ wide, 100% cotton fabrics. Measurements include ¼″ seam allowances.

Skip the Fat Quarters
When buying fabric for this quilt, ¼ yard cuts, not fat quarters, work best. Each quarter yard yields 10 to 11 elongated tumbler blocks, with very little leftover.

TEMPLATE E (page 79)

MAIN FABRIC: ¼ yard cuts each of 26 softly colored coordinating fabrics or equivalent from your stash

BACKING: 5 yards

BINDING: ¾ yard coordinating fabric

BATTING: 85″ × 88″

CUTTING THE FABRIC

For tips and tricks on cutting tumbler blocks see Cutting (page 22).

MAIN FABRIC

Cut 10 tumbler blocks from each of 26 fabrics using template E, for 260 blocks (130 pairs), or equivalent from your stash, keeping them in pairs.

Piecing the Quilt

1. Refer to the main quilt image for quilt block placement. Place the blocks on your design wall and spend some time moving them around to be sure colors are well distributed. The first and last rows will alternate single blocks with pairs. For guidance on arranging your blocks see Using a Design Wall (page 22).

2. When you are happy with all your fabric choices and your arrangement, it is time to move to your sewing machine. Begin piecing the blocks together. Working with 2 blocks at a time and replacing them on the design wall. Refer to Piecing the Quilt Top (page 23).

3. When the row is complete, press the seams in one direction. The seams of the next row should be pressed in the opposite direction.

4. Continue until all your rows are sewn. Check that you have pressed the seams in alternate directions one row to the next, then sew rows together.

Completing the Quilt

1. Using the guidance in Squaring the Quilt Top (page 24), trim the quilt to eliminate the partial blocks at the sides, and make any adjustments needed to be sure the quilt is squared up.

2. Layer the quilt top, batting, and backing.

3. Quilt as desired. I decided to have this quilted with soft vertical waves of parallel lines that enhance the overall look of the quilt and gently guide your eye through the quilt. For more information see Quilting (page 25).

4. Bind the quilt with a complementary fabric. For a refresher see Binding (page 26).

Why it Works

I used a soft, muted palette when selecting the blocks for this quilt, which produced a quiet, restful look that is perfect for a bedroom, to lull you off to sleep. It is the low contrast between the blocks that makes this work and would be just as successful using a set of deep, rich colors with low contrast between them.

EIGHT TOGETHER

As my collection of tumbler blocks grew and I moved them around on my design wall, I stumbled on this arrangement, which uses 8 blocks of the same fabric. Grouped together, they create a larger block, and open up a flood of possibilities. I found it was a great way to highlight some of my favorite fabrics and loved it instantly. I call it an "8-block."

I have made this quilt pattern in a wide variety of colors, many of them are variations on a monochromatic color scheme. What was my inspiration? I have my fabrics sorted by color. All I have to do is open a box of any color, and my fingers start to itch. How would all these fabrics look together on the design wall? Playing with the placement of the sets of 8 changes the look dramatically. Some ideas I played with include a gentle transition from one shade to another, a sharp contrast between each set, and grouping sets of 8 into super sets. So many possibilities with just one color!

I began by using 8 blocks cut from just template A, but quickly realized that the center sets of three would be a lot faster and easier to make if I had a second template to cut the equivalent of three tumbler blocks.

Three A blocks versus one B block cut from the same fabric

Two fabric sets from my stash.

Working With A and B Blocks

When you are joining rows together, it is important that template A is centered in the middle of template B. The simplest way to do this is to create a fold in both A and B blocks, either by finger pressing or with an iron. When you are sewing, simply align the fold lines and stitch.

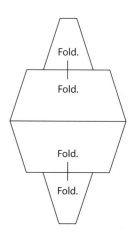

Pink Lemonade

| FINISHED SIZE: 49″ × 60″ |

I have always loved the color pink, but too much pink can be overwhelming. Could I find
a way to make an all-pink quilt that would not feel too girly girly? This quilt said yes and
started me on a voyage of monochromatic discovery. I used 72 different fabrics in this quilt,
from a wide range of light, mid and dark tones of the palest of pinks to magenta

MATERIALS

*Quantities are for 42/44″ wide, 100% cotton fabrics.
Measurements include ¼″ seam allowances.*

TEMPLATES A AND B (page 77)

MAIN FABRICS: 72 rectangles 8″ × 11″, or ⅛ yard
each of 72 light to dark pink to magenta fabrics

Skip the Scraps
From one fabric strip 3½″ × WOF (at least 38″), you can cut
4 template A and 4 template B tumbler blocks.

BACKING: 3¼ yards

BINDING: ½ yard coordinating fabric

BATTING: 57″ × 68″

CUTTING THE FABRIC

For tips and tricks on cutting tumbler blocks see Cutting
(page 22).

MAIN FABRICS

Cut 2 tumbler blocks using template A and
2 tumbler blocks using template B from each of
58 fabrics. Pin each 8-block set together as you
cut your fabrics to keep them organized. From
the remaining fabrics, cut 1 tumbler block using
template A and 1 tumbler block using template B.
You will need 58 full 8-blocks and 14 half blocks.

►CHANGING IT UP

Don't make me choose a favorite color... I love them all. I enjoyed this quilt so much I made it in a number of colorways, playing with placement of lights and darks in lots of different ways.

I used the same concept but now in purple, blue, and in another pink quilt. Notice how the placement of darker and lighter sets changes the whole look of the quilt.

Piecing the Quilt

1. Refer to the main quilt image for quilt block placement. Place the sets of blocks on your design wall to form the 8-blocks. Spend some time moving your sets around to be sure colors are well distributed. For guidance on arranging your blocks see Using a Design Wall (page 22).

2. When you are happy with all your fabric choices and your arrangement, it is time to move to your sewing machine. Referring to Piecing the Quilt Top (page 23), begin piecing the blocks together. Work with 2 blocks at a time, replacing them on the design wall.

3. When the row is complete, press the seams in one direction. The seams of the next row should be pressed in the opposite direction.

4. Continue until all your rows are sewn. Check that you have pressed the seams in alternate directions one row to the next, then sew rows together. When you are joining the rows together, it is important that template A is centered in the middle of template B, see Working with A and B Blocks (page 44).

Completing the Quilt

1. Using the guidance in Squaring the Quilt Top (page 24), trim the quilt to eliminate the partial blocks at the sides, and make any adjustments needed to be sure the quilt is squared up.

2. Layer the quilt top, batting, and backing.

3. Quilt as desired. I decided to have this quilted with parallel vertical lines that enhance the overall look of the quilt and gently guide your eye through the quilt. For more information see Quilting (page 25).

4. Bind the quilt with a complementary fabric. For a refresher see Binding (page 26).

Why it Works

I purposefully created a color gradient with my pink fabrics. The colors flow from very dark at the bottom of the quilt to the lightest tints at the top. Notice that values are fairly similar across the rows. This creates a lot of movement in your quilt top and draws your eye from the bottom to the top. You can achieve this look with any color. The trick is to keep similar values next to each other, getting slightly lighter with each grouping.

PINK LEMONADE

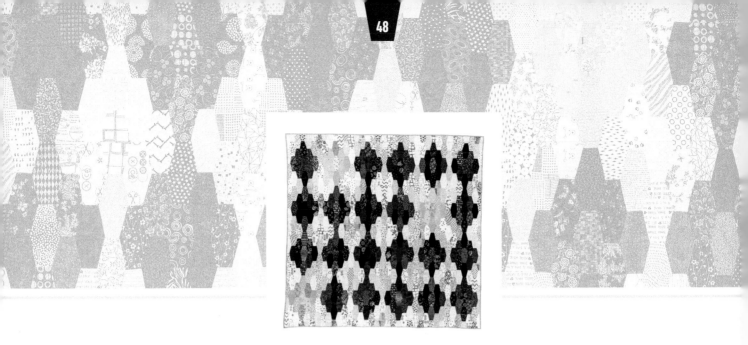

Not Just Black and White

FINISHED SIZE 73″ × 78″

There have been so many black and white fabrics for sale in the past few years, that I built up quite a stock. This quilt was a great opportunity for me to start using them. I expanded the tumbler design from 8 blocks together to 18 blocks and created this semi-scrappy version. I used pairs of fabric blocks to provide unity and prevent the quilt from being visually chaotic.

MATERIALS

Quantities are for 42/44″ wide, 100% cotton fabrics. Measurements include ¼″ seam allowances.

TEMPLATE A (page 77)

BLACK WITH WHITE OR GRAY PRINTS: 3 yards total

WHITE WITH BLACK OR GRAY PRINTS: 4 yards total

YELLOW-GOLD PRINTS: ⅝ yard total

BACKING: 4⅞ yards

BINDING: ¾ yard coordinating fabric

BATTING: 81″ × 86″

CUTTING THE FABRIC

For tips and tricks on cutting tumbler blocks see Cutting (page 22).

BLACK WITH WHITE OR GRAY

Cut 189 pairs of tumbler blocks (378 blocks total) using template A. Keep the pairs together and scatter the pairs through the quilt.

WHITE WITH BLACK OR GRAY

Cut 265 pairs of tumbler blocks (530 blocks total) using template A. Keep the pairs together and scatter the pairs through the quilt.

YELLOW-GOLD

Cut 27 pairs of tumbler blocks (54 blocks total) using template A.

NOT JUST BLACK AND WHITE

Piecing the Quilt

1. The first and last rows of this quilt are made of white print blocks only. Refer to the main quilt image for quilt block placement. Start building your blocks on your design wall, referring to the photo of the finished quilt for the layout. I placed a matching pair in the center of each set of 18 and distributed the other pairs around it to create symmetry around the center. For guidance on arranging your blocks see Using a Design Wall (page 22).

Eighteen set closeup

2. When you are happy with all your fabric choices and your arrangement, it is time to move to your sewing machine. Referring to Piecing the Quilt Top (page 23), begin piecing the blocks together, working with 2 blocks at a time, and replacing them on the design wall.

3. When the row is complete, press the seams in one direction. The seams of the next row should be pressed in the opposite direction.

4. Continue until all your rows are sewn. Check that you have pressed the seams in alternate directions from one row to the next, then sew rows together.

Completing the Quilt

1. Using the guidance in Squaring the Quilt Top (page 24), trim the quilt to eliminate the partial blocks at the sides, and make any adjustments needed to be sure the quilt is squared up.

2. Layer the quilt top, batting, and backing.

3. Quilt as desired. I used matchstick quilting in this quilt, matching the thread color to the block. Because I used a 50 wt thread, the quilting is barely noticeable, and allows the quilt design to shine. For more information see Quilting (page 25).

4. Bind the quilt with a complementary fabric. For a refresher see Binding (page 26).

Why it Works

This quilt is so successful because of the neutrals. Black and white are both neutrals, so you can add any color and it will really pop.

Getting Your Stripes On

| FINISHED SIZE 69″ × 78″ |

This quilt reminds me of Ikat carpets and is such a fun way to use those striped fabrics you have been collecting. Stripes often feature a range of colors in a single fabric, so they tend to go together easily. This design starts with the basic 8 blocks together, surrounded by a ring of contrasting blocks. Here you do not want the blocks to blend together, instead you are aiming for each set of blocks to be different and distinct from its neighbors. Notice that I didn't stick strictly to stripes. I included zigzags, plaids, and dotted fabrics too!

MATERIALS

Quantities are for 42/44″ wide, 100% cotton fabrics. Measurements include ¼″ seam allowances.

TEMPLATES A AND B (page 77)

ASSORTED STRIPED FABRICS: 6¼ yards total (Feel free to substitute dotted or zigzag fabrics in place of some of the stripes.)

BACKING: 5 yards

BINDING: ¾ yard coordinating fabric

BATTING: 77″ × 86″

CUTTING THE FABRIC

For tips and tricks on cutting tumbler blocks see Cutting (page 22).

ASSORTED STRIPED FABRICS

Cut 44 sets of 2 tumbler blocks with template A and 2 tumbler blocks with template B. Each set makes an 8-block. Pin each set together to keep them organized while you work.

Cut 5 sets of half blocks, which are composed of 1 tumbler block A and 1 tumbler block B. These are used in the top row of the quilt. Check the photo for placement.

Cut 44 sets of 10 tumbler blocks with template A. These sets surround the "8-blocks."

Cut 5 sets of 5 tumbler blocks with template A to surround the half blocks.

Cut extra quadruplets, triplets, pairs, and single tumbler blocks with template A to fill in as needed at the top, bottom, and sides of the quilt.

Piecing the Quilt

1. Start building your design, referring to the photo of the finished quilt for layout details. I started out by placing the 8-blocks on the design wall, and then auditioned the sets that surrounded them, looking for contrast. Keep playing until you are confident in your choices and arrangement. For guidance on arranging your blocks see Using a Design Wall (page 22).

2. When you are happy with all your fabric choices and your arrangement, it is time to move to your sewing machine. Referring to Piecing the Quilt Top (page 23), begin piecing the blocks together, working with 2 blocks at a time, and replacing them on the design wall.

3. When the row is complete, press the seams in one direction. The seams of the next row should be pressed in the opposite direction. Continue until all your rows are sewn.

4. Check that you have pressed the seams in alternate directions one row to the next, then sew the rows together.

Completing the Quilt

1. Using the guidance in Squaring the Quilt Top (page 24), trim the quilt to eliminate the partial blocks at the sides, and make any adjustments needed to be sure the quilt is squared up.

2. Layer the quilt top, batting, and backing.

3. Quilt as desired. I used horizontal lines, spaced one inch apart on this quilt. Don't stress about the thread color. I chose a 50 wt. tan colored thread and the quilting is barely noticeable and allows the quilt design to shine. For more information see Quilting (page 25).

4. Bind the quilt with a complementary fabric. For a refresher see Binding (page 26).

Why it Works

The fabrics I used had a range of colors and designs. There were wide stripes, narrow stripes, some in subtle color variations, and others in bold contrasting colors. Darker tones were placed next to lighter or brighter ones. This variety helped each fabric stand out from its neighbor to the visual interest to the quilt.

ADDING A SPACER

Designing new quilts is all about experimenting. I had been playing a lot with monochromatic arrangements of tumbler blocks and loved the look of colors flowing into one another. But now I wondered if there was a way to separate the sets of color from each other. I eventually came up with the idea of a spacer block, so I made a template, and began to play.

Working with Spacer Blocks

Spacer blocks can be used to create space between tumbler blocks in your quilt. There are a few things to remember when working with these blocks, however. They have the same width top and bottom as the tumbler block and use the same angle but they are not symmetrical. If you accidentally rotate the block 90°, the measurements are slightly different and will cause problems when piecing. Mark the bottom of each block using a heat—or water-removable marker pen or pencil. When you are sewing your blocks together, be sure these marks are at the bottom or your block—never at the sides.

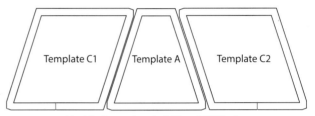

Mark bottom edge of all C1 and C2 blocks.

Baby Blue

| FINISHED SIZE: 47″ × 54″ |

Soft shades of color on a baby blue background give off a calming vibe in this quilt,
and using solid fabrics allows for a harlequin design to emerge.

MATERIALS

Quantities are for 42/44″ wide, 100% cotton fabrics. Measurements include ¼″ seam allowances.

TEMPLATES A, B, C1, AND C2 (**pages** 77 and 78)

FABRIC N: 2½ yards light blue for background and binding

FABRIC A: ½ yard

FABRICS B, C, AND H: ⅜ yard each (refer to chart below for colors)

FABRICS D–G AND I–M: ¼ yard each

BACKING: 3⅛ yards

BATTING: 55″ × 62″

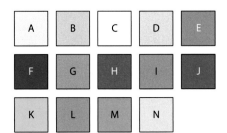

CUTTING THE FABRIC

For tips and tricks on cutting tumbler blocks see Cutting (page 22). For marking the C1 and C2 blocks, see Working with Spacer Blocks (page 54).

FABRIC N

Cut 54 blocks with template C1, 54 blocks with template C2, and 18 tumbler blocks with template B. Be sure to mark the bottom edge of each C1 and C2 block. Check that this mark is at the bottom of the block (not the sides) when piecing. The B blocks will be used at one end of each row.

FABRIC A

Cut 9 tumbler blocks with template A and 9 tumbler blocks with template B. Refer to Skip the Scraps (page 45)

FABRICS B AND C

Cut 6 tumbler blocks with template A and 6 tumbler blocks with template B.

FABRIC H AND J

Cut 5 tumbler blocks with template A and 5 tumbler blocks with template B.

FABRICS D, I, AND K

Cut 4 tumbler blocks with template A and 4 tumbler blocks with template B.

FABRIC E

Cut 3 tumbler blocks with template A and 3 tumbler blocks with template B.

FABRIC F, G, L, AND M

Cut 2 tumbler blocks with template A and 2 tumbler blocks with template B.

CHANGING IT UP

The spacer block allows a lot of freedom in color choices, so be bold! Play with a wide mix of fabrics in the blocks, and don't forget to try different fabrics for the spacers. The spacers really unify the quilt, but that doesn't mean they need to be quiet!

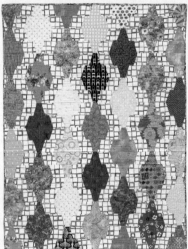

Piecing the Quilt

1. Place the blocks on your design wall. Refer to the main quilt image for quilt block placement. For guidance on arranging your blocks see Using a Design Wall (page 22).

2. When you are happy with all your fabric choices and your arrangement, it is time to move to your sewing machine. Referring to Piecing the Quilt Top (page 23), begin piecing the blocks together, working with 2 blocks at a time, and replacing them on the design wall. For a refresher on making sure your blocks line up, review Working With A and B Blocks (page 44).

3. When the row is complete, press the seams in one direction. The seams of the next row should be pressed in the opposite direction. Continue until all your rows are sewn.

4. Check that you have pressed the seams in alternate directions one row to the next, then sew the rows together.

Completing the Quilt

1. Using the guidance in Squaring the Quilt Top (page 24), trim the quilt to eliminate the partial blocks at the sides, and make any adjustments needed to be sure the quilt is squared up.

2. Layer the quilt top, batting, and backing.

3. Quilt as desired. I chose to highlight the various parts of this quilt with different designs, using white thread throughout, but would look just as stunning with simple straight horizontal line quilting on the entire piece. For more information see Quilting (page 25).

4. Bind the quilt with the blue background fabric. For a refresher see Binding (page 26).

Why it Works

Many of the colors used in this quilt are considered neutrals; white, cream, beige, grays, and black. Neutrals are great to use in a quilt, as they work in combination with a wide range of colors. Because they range from light to dark in this quilt, they provide interesting contrast and move your eye around the quilt. The remaining colors chosen for this design are muted tones, meaning a bit of gray is added to generate these colors. This helps to provide harmony in the quilt.

BABY BLUE

Magenta Jam

| FINISHED SIZE: 58″ × 72″ |

Here is a totally different look from the previous quilt. I added another set of tumbler blocks around the center eight and again used solid fabrics, which give great color contrast. The background color is a bold magenta which is separated from the red-brown center 8 groups with colors chosen to stand out.

MATERIALS

Quantities are for 42/44″ wide, 100% cotton fabrics. Measurements include ¼″ seam allowances.

TEMPLATES A, B, C1, AND C2 (pages 77 and 78)

MAGENTA: 3 yards for background and binding

DARK-RED BROWN: 1½ yards

ASSORTED SOLIDS: ⅓ yard each of 14 in a range of colors (See chart below.)

BACKING: 3¾ yards

BATTING: 66″ × 80″

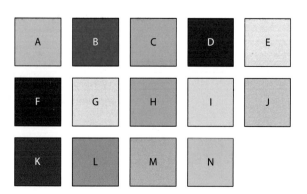

CUTTING THE FABRIC

For tips and tricks on cutting tumbler blocks see Cutting (page 22). For marking the C1 and C2 blocks, see Working with Spacer Blocks (page 54).

MAGENTA

Cut 108 blocks using template C1 and 108 blocks using template C2. Be sure to mark the bottom edge of each block. Check that this mark is at the bottom of the block (not the sides) when piecing.

RED-BROWN

Cut 48 tumbler blocks with template A and 48 blocks with template B.

FABRICS A AND F

Cut 30 tumbler blocks using template A.

FABRICS B, D, E, G, AND K

Cut 20 tumbler blocks using template A.

FABRICS C AND I

Cut 15 tumbler blocks using template A.

FABRICS H, J, L, M, AND N

Cut 10 tumbler blocks using template A.

Piecing the Quilt

1. Refer to the main quilt image for quilt block placement. Place the blocks on your design wall. Spend some time moving your blocks around to be sure colors are well distributed. For guidance on arranging your blocks see Using a Design Wall (page 22). Add the magenta background pieces between the blocks and at the end of each row.

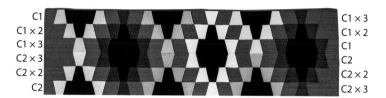

C1
C1 × 2
C1 × 3
C2 × 3
C2 × 2
C2

C1 × 3
C1 × 2
C1
C2
C2 × 2
C2 × 3

2. When you are happy with all your fabric choices and your arrangement, it is time to move to your sewing machine. Referring to Piecing the Quilt Top (page 23), begin piecing the blocks together, working with 2 blocks at a time, and replacing them on the design wall.

3. When the row is complete, press the seams in one direction. The seams of the next row should be pressed in the opposite direction. Continue until all your rows are sewn.

4. Check that you have pressed the seams in alternate directions one row to the next, then sew rows together. When you are joining the rows together, it is important that template A is centered in the middle of template B, for a refresher on how to do this see Working With A and B Blocks (page 44).

Completing the Quilt

1. Using the guidance in Squaring the Quilt Top (page 24), trim the quilt to eliminate the partial blocks at the sides, and make any adjustments needed to be sure the quilt is squared up.

2. Layer the quilt top, batting, and backing.

3. Quilt as desired. I chose to highlight the various parts of this quilt with different designs, using white thread throughout, but would look just as stunning with simple straight horizontal line quilting on the entire piece. For more information see Quilting (page 25).

4. Bind the quilt with the magenta background fabric. For a refresher see Binding (page 26).

▶ CHANGING IT UP

You get a different look when you mix solids and patterned fabrics, as shown in the sample below. The solid fabrics have a strong voice in the quilts and are the first thing your eye sees. Hmmm... what would this look like as a totally scrappy quilt?

This version uses a tiny floral print for the center of the block, and the colors of the surrounding sets were chosen from that print.

Subtle patterned fabrics can be used for the background and the center of the blocks, allowing the blocks surrounding the centers to stand out.

Why it Works

The fabrics in this quilt are all solids, and the background is rich and bold. Solid fabrics help the groups of blocks stand out from each other, and the color contrasts contribute to the dynamic look of the quilt. The center eight blocks are all the same color and help bring harmony to the quilt.

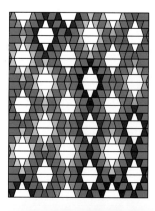

FROM THE BED TO THE WALL

There are so many different types of art quilts, and we all probably have our own idea of what an art quilt is. Art quilts can be pictorial, featuring a realistic or stylized depiction of people or trees or buildings, for example. The quilts I have created with the tumbler block are more abstract or impressionistic. The tumbler block shape creates movement, directing your eye in areas of contrast, and virtually disappears in areas of low contrast. They are value and color studies inspired more by memories of natural elements such as water, forests, and sunsets than by literal interpretations from photos.

The quilts in this section I consider more art quilts than bed quilts. I have them hanging in my living room, hall, and bedroom where I often find myself spending time looking at them, and my eye explores something different each time.

If you are interested in trying this type of quilt, a photo you love can be a great place to start. But don't be afraid to veer from the plan as you start to build your piece. Both areas of blended values and higher contrast make the work dynamic and interesting. The patterns in your fabric help create value changes, and your personal stash will influence how much blending versus contrast you have in your quilt.

The darkest areas of the quilt are what draw your eye in immediately, before you start to expand and explore the rest of the piece. A good place to start is with these darker areas. Remember that value is more important here than color, and you can place dark brown, purples and greens next to each other and still achieve a natural flow. My pieces place the darkest areas slightly off-center and become lighter near the outer edges of the quilt.

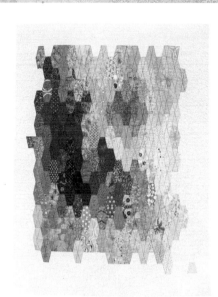

Fire

| FINISHED SIZE: 48″ × 72″ |

Bright reds, oranges, and yellows conjure up images of an intensely burning fire, placed here on a calming background of white. This quilt was inspired by photos of flames. Each pair of blocks is a different fabric, so only a small amount is needed. I have provided a rough estimate of how many blocks of each color is required, but this will partly depend on your fabric supply. Remember to swap with or borrow from friends to find colors you are short of!

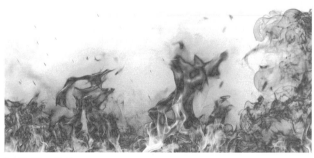

Inspiration photos

MATERIALS

Quantities are for 42/44″ wide, 100% cotton fabrics. Measurements include ¼″ seam allowances.

TEMPLATE A (page 77)

YELLOW: 65 rectangles 5″ × 8″ from palest yellow to deep gold and orange-gold

RED: 25 rectangles 5″ × 8″ red fabric from red-orange to red and magenta

ORANGE: 27 rectangles of 5″ × 8″ from pale coral to deep orange

PINK: 47 rectangles of 5″ × 8″ from palest to deep pink

WHITE: 2½ yards for background and binding

BACKING: 3⅛ yards

BATTING: 56″ × 80″

FIRE

CUTTING THE FABRIC

For tips and tricks on cutting tumbler blocks see Cutting (page 22).

YELLOW, RED, ORANGE, PINK

Cut 2 tumbler blocks using template A. Keep color groups in separate piles to make arranging blocks on your design wall easier.

WHITE

From the length of the fabric, cut 2 rectangles 6″ × 49″ for the top and bottom borders. Cut 1 rectangle 3½″ × 39″ for the bottom pieced row.

Cut 39 rectangles 3½″ × 10″. These will be used at the ends of each row. Trim one end of each rectangle using template A, as you fit them to the neighboring tumbler block. If you are using a solid colored fabric, you can trim them all identical, and flip them to fit where needed. These rectangles will be trimmed on the straight end when you are ready to square up the quilt.

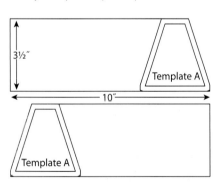

Cut 15 tumbler blocks using template A. Refer to the quilt photo for placement

Piecing the Quilt

1. Refer to the main quilt image for quilt block placement. Place the blocks on your design wall. I started with the pale pink blocks and worked out and upward. Spend some time moving your blocks around to be sure colors are well distributed with areas blending and areas of contrast. Try to avoid all the blocks at the edges being in one line. Occasionally place an extra white or colored block at one end to help randomize the distribution. Notice in the white area near the pink section I placed one very pale pink block—it takes a while to see it! This bottom pieced row uses the white 3½″ × 39″ rectangle, 2 pink tumbler blocks, 2 white tumbler blocks, and 1 white rectangle 3½″ × 10″. For guidance on arranging your blocks see Using a Design Wall (page 22).

2. When you are happy with all your fabric choices and your arrangement, it is time to move to your sewing machine. Referring to Piecing the Quilt Top (page 23), begin piecing the blocks together, working with 2 blocks at a time, and replacing them on the design wall.

3. When the row is complete, press the seams in one direction. The seams of the next row should be pressed in the opposite direction. Continue until all your rows are sewn.

4. Check that you have pressed the seams in alternate directions one row to the next, then sew the rows together.

Completing the Quilt

1. Using the guidance in Squaring the Quilt Top (page 24), trim the quilt to eliminate the partial blocks at the sides, and make any adjustments needed to be sure the quilt is squared up.

2. Layer the quilt top, batting, and backing.

3. Quilt as desired. I chose to highlight the various parts of this quilt with different designs, using white thread and a swirly design in the white areas, and red thread and diagonal lines in the areas of color. For more information see Quilting (page 25).

4. Bind the quilt with the white background fabric. For a refresher see Binding (page 26).

Why it Works

The bright colors used in this quilt blend together in some areas, and contrast in others, providing lots of visual interest. The shift from reds to golds and pinks mimic colors seen in the inspiration images and give a sense of movement and immediacy to the quilt. The white borders help tone down the overall brightness of the quilt, and at the same time pull the overall design together.

Forest

| FINISHED SIZE: 47″ × 72″ |

All the colors that nature provides in gardens, parks, and forests were the inspiration for this quilt. Each pair of blocks is a different fabric, so only a small amount of each is needed. Remember to swap or borrow from friends to find fabrics in colors you want more of! Most of the fabrics in this quilt are print fabrics but most are low contrast prints or tone-on-tone fabrics.

Inspiration photos

MATERIALS

Quantities are for 42/44″ wide, 100% cotton fabrics. Measurements include ¼″ seam allowances.

TEMPLATE A (page 77)

ASSORTED FABRICS: Approximately 280 rectangles 5″ × 8″ in range of colors from creams, light grays, lime, yellow, teal, brown, mid to dark greens, and dark blue

BACKING: 3⅛ yards

BINDING: ⅝ yard coordinating fabric

BATTING: 55″ × 80″

CUTTING THE FABRIC

For tips and tricks on cutting tumbler blocks see Cutting (page 22).

ASSORTED FABRICS

Cut 2 tumbler blocks using template A from each fabric. I cut a total of 300 pairs of blocks and used 288 in the quilt. It is always good to have some options ready before you start. Keep color groups in separate piles to make arranging blocks on your design wall easier.

Piecing the Quilt

1. Refer to the main quilt image for quilt block placement. Place the blocks on your design wall. I started with the center dark green blocks and worked outward, then added blocks working up and down at the same time. For guidance on arranging your blocks see Using a Design Wall (page 22).

2. When you are happy with all your fabric choices and your arrangement, it is time to move to your sewing machine. Referring to Piecing the Quilt Top (page 23), begin piecing the blocks together, working with 2 blocks at a time, and replacing them on the design wall.

3. When the row is complete, press the seams in one direction. The seams of the next row should be pressed in the opposite direction. Continue until all your rows are sewn.

4. Check that you have pressed the seams in alternate directions one row to the next, then sew the rows together.

Completing the Quilt

1. Using the guidance in Squaring the Quilt Top (page 24), trim the quilt to eliminate the partial blocks at the sides, and make any adjustments needed to be sure the quilt is squared up.

2. Layer the quilt top, batting, and backing.

3. Quilt as desired. Because the colors in this quilt are fairly dark, and there is quite a bit of pattern in the blocks, I chose to have it quilted with uneven wavy lines, which help add movement to the quilt. For more information see Quilting (page 25).

4. Bind with a fabric that complements the quilt. For a refresher see Binding (page 26).

Why it Works

The wide range of colors used in this quilt were positioned to blend from one to another, with little sharp contrast between blocks. Your eye is immediately drawn to the darkest areas of the quilt, then moves to the bright lime and yellow areas, and finally starts to explore the rest of the piece.

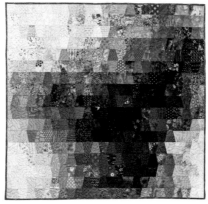

Blue Ocean

| FINISHED SIZE: 49″ × 51″ |

This quilt induces a zen-like feeling of calm and ease to me, along with a touch of mystery. It was inspired by my memories of scuba diving in the Caribbean. I was near the surface of the water, at the edge of an underwater cliff that dropped 6000 ft. That depth was the deepest blue I had ever seen—amazing! I chose colors ranging from the softest of blues and grays to deepest of blues. Each block is a different fabric, so only a small amount of each is needed.

MATERIALS

Quantities are for 42/44″ wide, 100% cotton fabrics. Measurements include ¼″ seam allowances.

TEMPLATE A (page 77)

ASSORTED FABRICS: Approximately 425 scraps at least 3½″ × 3½″ in a range of colors from creams, light grays, and all shades of blue to purple

BACKING: 3¼ yards

BINDING: ½ yard matching fabric

BATTING: 57″ × 59″

CUTTING THE FABRIC

For tips and tricks on cutting tumbler blocks see Cutting (page 22).

ASSORTED FABRICS

Cut 1 tumbler block from each fabric with template A, you will need 425 total. I cut 450 blocks so I'd have some options ready before starting. Keep the lighter and darker shades in separate piles. This makes arranging blocks on your design wall later much easier.

Piecing the Quilt

1. Refer to the main quilt image for quilt block placement. Place the blocks on your design wall. I started with the center darkest blue blocks and worked outward from there. Don't be afraid to add an occasional block of a different color—check out the magenta block buried in with the darkest of purples. For guidance on arranging your blocks see Using a Design Wall (page 22).

2. When you are happy with all your fabric choices and your arrangement, it is time to move to your sewing machine. Referring to Piecing the Quilt Top (page 23), begin piecing the blocks together, working with 2 blocks at a time, and replacing them on the design wall.

3. When the row is complete, press the seams in one direction. The seams of the next row should be pressed in the opposite direction. Continue until all your rows are sewn.

4. Check that you have pressed the seams in alternate directions one row to the next, then sew the rows together.

Completing the Quilt

1. Using the guidance in Squaring the Quilt Top (page 24), trim the quilt to eliminate the partial blocks at the sides, and make any adjustments needed to be sure the quilt is squared up.

2. Layer the quilt top, batting, and backing.

3. Quilt as desired. Because the colors in this quilt are fairly dark, and there is quite a bit of pattern in the blocks, I chose to have it quilted with a meandering stitch reminiscent of contour lines, to reinforce the idea of depth. These mostly disappear in the darker areas of the quilt but are more visible in the lighter areas. For more information see Quilting (page 25).

4. Bind the quilt with a complementary fabric. For a refresher see Binding (page 26).

Why it Works

This quilt features a narrow range of colors, but these vary a lot in value. The blocks were positioned to blend from one to another, with little sharp contrast between blocks. Most of the fabrics in this quilt have some pattern in them, and this adds visual interest, but from a distance they read as solids. Your eye is immediately drawn to the darkest areas of the quilt, moves to single magenta block, and then begins to explore other areas of the quilt.

Search online for images of water for even more inspiration.

Sunrise

| FINISHED SIZE: 55″ × 48″ |

Haven't we all taken tons of photos of sunrise and sunset, trying to capture those
magical moments of the day when the sky turns shades of yellow and gold?

MATERIALS

*Quantities are for 42/44″ wide, 100% cotton fabrics.
Measurements include ¼″ seam allowances.*

I used mostly fabrics that read as solids.

TEMPLATE F (page 79)

WHITE, CREAM, GRAY, BLUE: 72 rectangles at least 4″ × 12″
in off-white, creams, light grays, and blues for the sky

YELLOW, GOLD: 52 rectangles at least 4″ × 12″
blocks of softest yellows to gold

BROWNS: 14 rectangles at least 4″ × 12″ blocks
in shades of medium to dark brown

BACKING: 3⅛ yards

BINDING: ½ yard

BATTING: 63″ × 56″

CUTTING THE FABRIC

For tips and tricks on cutting tumbler blocks see Cutting
(page 22).

WHITE, CREAM, GRAY, BLUE

Cut 1 pair of tumbler blocks from each fabric with
template F, for a total of 72 pairs. Keep each color
group in a separate pile. This makes arranging
blocks on your design wall later much easier.

YELLOW, GOLD

Cut 1 pair of tumbler blocks from each fabric
with template F, for a total of 52 pairs. Keep
each color group in a separate pile.

BROWNS

Cut 1 pair of tumbler blocks from each fabric
with template F, for a total of 14 pairs. Keep
each color group in a separate pile.

Piecing the Quilt

1. Refer to the main quilt image for quilt block placement. Place the blocks on your design wall. I started with the brown mountains at the bottom of the piece and worked upward from there. Spend some time moving your blocks around so that the blocks blend 1 to the next. It is a good idea to step back to look at your work as you build it or take a photo with your camera. You can then get a good overall sense of the way the gradient of dark to light is working.For guidance on arranging your blocks see Using a Design Wall (page 22).

2. When you are happy with all your fabric choices and your arrangement, it is time to move to your sewing machine. Referring to Piecing the Quilt Top (page 23), begin piecing the blocks together, working with 2 blocks at a time, and replacing them on the design wall.

3. When the row is complete, press the seams in one direction. The seams of the next row should be pressed in the opposite direction. Continue until all your rows are sewn.

4. Check that you have pressed the seams in alternate directions one row to the next, then sew the rows together.

Completing the Quilt

1. Using the guidance in Squaring the Quilt Top (page 24), trim the quilt to eliminate the partial blocks at the sides, and make any adjustments needed to be sure the quilt is squared up.

2. Layer the quilt top, batting, and backing.

3. Quilt as desired. This quilt was quilted with several different designs. Swirls and cloud-like shapes for the sky, diagonal waves for the sunset yellow area, and horizontal waves in the browns of the mountain. For more information see Quilting (page 25).

4. I folded my binding completely to the back of the quilt like a facing. If you prefer a traditional binding, bind the quilt with a complementary fabric. For a refresher see Binding (page 26).

Why it Works

The blocks in this quilt were positioned to flow from one to another, minimizing contrast between blocks. The horizontal layout reflects what clouds in the sky and a sun setting behind mountains look like in nature, and thus entirely natural. Your eye is immediately drawn to the darkest area of the quilt and then begins to explore other areas of the quilt, studying the darker clouds in the sky.

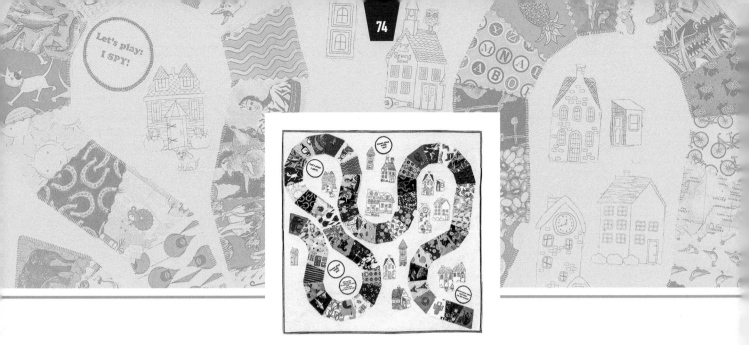

Bonus Project: Come Play With Me

| FINISHED SIZE: 37″ × 37″ |

This quilt is perfect for tummy time, playing I spy, and even a simple game. Young babies need to be placed on their tummies to gain the strength to hold up their heads and having something fun to look at encourages that. When older, you can point to things and the child can name them. Later, you can play I Spy. The sinuous curves can be used as a motorway for cars or a road for dolls to stroll. As they get older still, get out the dice! Roll one and move that number of spaces. Land on red, roll again and move forward that number of squares. Land on black, roll again and move back that number of spaces. Remember: Land on *red*, move ahead, land on *black* you must go back.

MATERIALS

Quantities are for 42/44″ wide, 100% cotton fabrics. Measurements include ¼″ seam allowances.

TEMPLATE G (page 79)

ASSORTED FABRICS: 56 charm squares or equivalent in 5″ squares, each featuring a fun image. I included 6 fabrics that read as black, and 6 fabrics that read as red.

I added a variety of fussy-cut images of houses and text saying Come Play with Me, Let's Play, I Spy, etc. to the background. I printed these onto fabric with my inkjet printer and fused them into the background. You may also appliqué images from other fabric or use a printed background.

BACKGROUND: 1⅛ yards

BACKING: 1¼ yards

ADDITIONAL FABRIC IMAGES FOR BACKGROUND APPLIQUÉS (optional)

505 TEMPORARY ADHESIVE FABRIC SPRAY

BINDING: ½ yard coordinating fabric

BATTING: 45″ × 45″

CUTTING THE FABRIC

For tips and tricks on cutting tumbler blocks see Cutting (page 22).

ASSORTED FABRICS

Cut 1 tumbler block from each fabric using template G.

Piecing the Quilt

This quilt is made in a less traditional way than most quilts.

1. Create a quilt sandwich with the background fabric, batting and backing fabric and quilt it in an all-over quilt design. I used a very close meandering stitch to give the quilt some strength and rigidity.

2. Take your tumbler blocks and play with them on your design wall until you are happy with all your fabric choices and your arrangement. I used 56 blocks in this quilt, but you may have a different arrangement and use more or fewer. Refer to the main quilt image for quilt block placement. For guidance on arranging your blocks see Using a Design Wall (page 22).

3. Sew the blocks together, two at a time, returning them to the design wall. Continue until your tumbler blocks are all joined.

4. Spray the reverse side of the tumbler blocks with 505 temporary fabric adhesive. Carefully lay the blocks onto the background fabric.

5. Appliqué the blocks to the background fabric with either a straight or zigzag stitch.

6. Optional: If you are adding additional images to the background as I did, spray each one with the 505 temporary fabric adhesive and place on the background. Appliqué the images to the background with either a straight or zigzag stitch.

Completing the Quilt

1. Square the quilt top.

2. Bind the quilt with a complementary fabric. For a refresher see Binding (page 26). You are done!

TEMPLATE PATTERNS

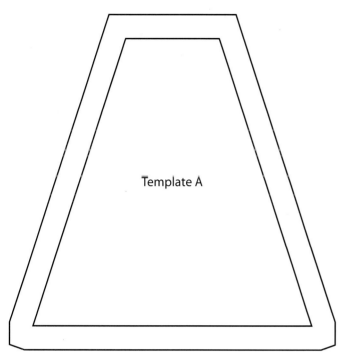

Template A

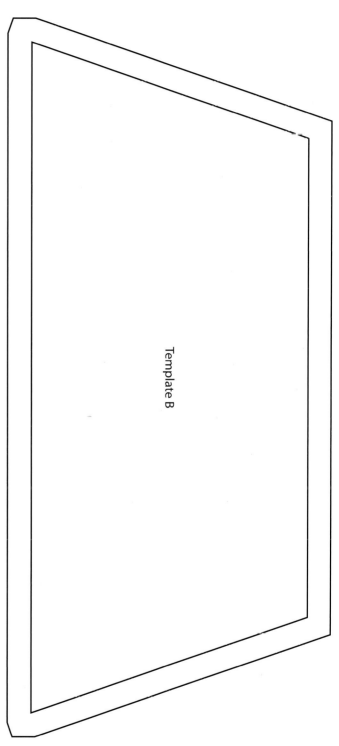

Template B

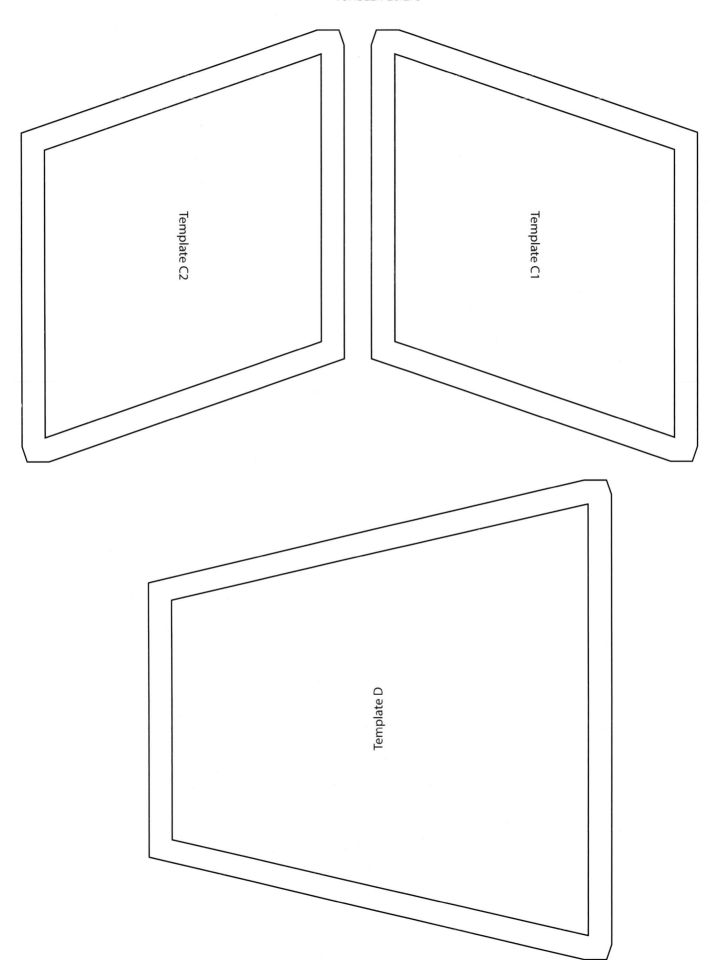

Template C2

Template C1

Template D

Template E

Template F

Template G

About the Author

My love of quilts and quilting begins and ends with colour. I've always LOVED colour. There were 5 children in our family, and my mother gave us each a different coloured bath towel. I loved seeing them all lined up on the clothesline! I drooled over those 72 coloured pencil sets, and a favourite image in colouring books was Joseph and his coat of many colours, giving you permission to use all the crayons in the box.

My working life was in research in science. This work encourages experimenting: always learning, making changes, and trying new things, and this carried over to my life outside of work. I always did something creative on the side.

I had a long and circuitous route to quilting. There were no quilters in the family, and I don't think I saw a quilt until I was in my 30s. I discovered Kaffe Fassett when he published his first knitting book. Inspired by his bright bold use of pattern and design, I set up a part-time knitting business, designing and selling sweater kits for babies and children. This was before digital cameras, colour photocopies, and online sales and was so satisfying creatively, but also very time-consuming. Kaffe moved into quilting, and I got interested. Then a new quilt shop opened near me, and I kept dropping by to drool over the fabric. I decided to take the plunge and sold my yarn stock to make room for fabric. Right from the start I was drawn to simple designs that let me play with colour.

I am an organizer too! I love to develop an idea and bring it to fruition, keeping things as streamlined and simple as possible. One of my ventures was Quilts at the Creek, an outdoor quilt show that ran for eight years in Toronto Canada. This show was meant for ALL quilters, and ran with a small group of committed volunteers. Thousands of people came one weekend every summer with three hundred quilts hung throughout an historic village at the edge of the city. More recently, I began an online ZOOM series bringing international quilt professionals to quilters everywhere. QuiltTalk was a great success, and such fun. However, as more and more ZOOM talks became available for quilters, I decided to end this venture, to give myself more time to focus on quilting- and this book!.